Babi Yar and Other Poems

Babi Yar and Other Poems

Ilya Ehrenburg

translated by
Anna Krushelnitskaya

Smokestack Books
School Farm
Nether Silton
North Yorkshire
YO7 2JZ.

e-mail: info@smokestack-books.co.uk

www.smokestack-books.co.uk

Russian text copyright
© Ilya Ehrenburg estate,
all rights reserved.

Published by
arrangement with
ELKOST International Literary Agency.

Translations
copyright 2024,
Anna Krushelnitskaya

Introduction
copyright 2024,
Joshua Rubenstein

ISBN 978-1-7394734-1-9

Smokestack Books
is represented by
Inpress Ltd

Содержание

Я скажу вам о детстве ушедшем, о маме...	26
Мне никто не скажет за уроком «слушай»...	28
Как скучно в «одиночке», вечер длинный...	30
Если ты к земле приложишь ухо...	32
О маме	34
Вздохи из чужбины	36
Канун	40
Прогулка	42
Молитва о России	44
Осенью 1918 года	50
Из желтой глины, из праха, из пыли...	52
Весна снега ворочала...	56
Бой быков	58
Русский в Андалузии	60
Не торопясь, внимательный биолог...	62
На ладони – карта, с малолетства...	64
Ты тронул ветку, ветка зашумела...	66
Додумать не дай, оборви, молю, этот голос...	68
Верность	70
Бродят Рахили, Хаимы, Лии...	72
Крылья выдумав, ушел под землю...	74
Есть в хаосе самом высокий строй...	76
Убей!	78
Ненависть	80
Есть время камни собирать,...	82
Бабий Яр	84
Когда я был молод, была уж война...	86
Я смутно жил и неуверенно...	88

Contents

Joshua Rubenstein, 'Poetry and Ilya Ehrenburg'...	13
I'll talk of past childhood, of Mamma...	27
There's no-one to say, like back in class, 'stop acting funny!'...	29
So bored in solitary, and the day won't end...	31
If you press your ear down to the ground	33
About Mamma	35
Sighs from Abroad	37
The Eve	39
A Stroll	43
A Prayer for Russia	45
Autumn of 1918	49
Out of yellow clay, out of dust, out of ashes...	53
Spring pushed around her snowfalls...	57
The Bullfight	59
A Russian in Andalusia	61
A studious biologist, enraptured...	63
Read your palm – a map, where every river...	65
You touched a branch; the branch awoke with rustling...	67
Don't let me finish this, banish this voice, perish the thought...	69
Faithfulness	71
A great many Leahs, Haims, Rahels...	73
I made up wings and vanished underground...	75
Chaos itself conceals an artful plan...	77
Kill!	79
Hatred	81
There is a time to gather stones...	83
Babi Yar	85
When I was a young man, we were in a war...	87
I lived my life unsurely, timidly...	89

Чужое горе – оно как овод...	90
9 Мая 1945	92
Был тихий день обычной осени,...	96
Дождь в Нагасаки	98
Верность...	100
Самый верный	102
Да разве могут дети юга	104
Я слышу все – и горестные шепоты...	106
Коровы в Калькутте	108
Морили прежде в розницу,...	110
Последняя любовь	114
В Доме литераторов	116
Зверинец	120
Из поэмы «Старость»	122

A grief not your own is a gadfly...	91
9 May 1945	93
It was a usual quiet autumn day...	97
Nagasaki Rain	99
Faithfulness...	101
The Most Faithful	103
How could the children of the South	105
I hear it all – the whispering, the whimpering...	107
The Cows of Calcutta	109
Old deaths came at a slower rate...	111
Last Love	115
At The House of Writers	117
The Menagerie	121
from 'Old Age'	123
Notes	124
Acknowledgements	126

Poetry and Ilya Ehrenburg

The career of Ilya Ehrenburg, the most renowned Soviet journalist of his generation, challenges our assumptions about collaboration, dissent, and survival. Born into a Jewish family in Kyiv in 1891, Ehrenburg lived through the greatest calamities of the twentieth century, including World War I, the Bolshevik revolution, the Spanish Civil War, Stalin's purges, World War II, and the Cold War. He was often on the front lines and almost everything he wrote made someone angry. Orthodox Marxist critics hated his novels in the 1920s. The Nazis burned his books in the 1930s. During World War II his columns against the Germans were so powerful that Hitler blamed Ehrenburg for German military defeats.[1] Then during the Cold War Ehrenburg was notorious for his attacks on American culture. A public figure as much as he was a writer, poet, and journalist, Ehrenburg made calculated, personal decisions within crisis after crisis in European and Soviet history. He managed to survive Stalin, but in spite of his official conformity there was always a feeling about Ehrenburg that he was different. Nadezhda Mandelstam, the widow of the martyred poet Osip Mandelstam, had this in mind when she dubbed him 'the odd man out' among Soviet writers. 'He was as helpless as everybody else,' she recalled about the Stalin era, 'but at least he tried to do something for others.'[2]

For half a century Ehrenburg's life abounded in controversy and contradiction. As a teenager, he both joined and left the Bolshevik party, only to make himself useful to Stalin decades later as an emissary to European intellectuals. While other Soviet writers were disappearing, Ehrenburg carried out political assignments living in France, traveling widely and still publishing in Moscow. Such privileges, alongside his evident adaptability, raised suspicions about Ehrenburg's motives and integrity. As a Jew, he was said to have betrayed his people; as a writer, his talent; and as a man, to have kept silent about Stalin's crimes and served the dictator solely to curry and enjoy the Kremlin's favor.

But a closer, most informed examination of Ehrenburg's life reveals a determined consistency that the seismic shifts of history have always, in Ehrenburg's case, obscured. Western and Soviet detractors have ignored his acts of independence from Stalin's policies, his anguished response to the Holocaust and lifelong opposition to anti-Semitism, and his importance to millions of Soviet citizens who revered him for trying to sustain Russia's connection to European art and culture. In the confused years after the Bolshevik revolution, in the terrifying quarter century under Stalin, and the breathless, liberating, and ultimately frustrating decade under Khrushchev, Ehrenburg was courageous, at times even outspoken when *no one* of similar stature dared to voice independent views.

Ilya Ehrenburg was not a rebellious martyr. Ironically, he began his public activism as a teenage member of Moscow's Bolshevik underground. Imprisoned in 1908 at the age of seventeen for eight months, he fled tsarist Russia for Paris, where he quickly joined other political émigrés. He also met Vladimir Lenin who was eager to learn about Ehrenburg's experience in the Bolshevik underground. But this kind of life could not sustain his interest. He saw how these émigrés cut themselves off from the broader life of Paris and how ideological fervor generated inflexibility, intolerance, and for him, boredom.

Ehrenburg signalled his break with the Bolsheviks by ridiculing Lenin in a satirical journal he himself edited. He soon began devoting all his energy to art and literature. In the West he is remembered as an accomplished journalist and novelist, but he actually began his literary career as a poet. Between 1910 and 1916, still living in Paris, Ehrenburg published several small volumes of poetry. Often he had to pay for the printing himself, then send copies to Russian poets, hoping for a critical response. At that time he was attracted to Roman Catholicism. He painted several icons and even considered converting, a spiritual step he ultimately abandoned. Nonetheless, his first collection, entitled *Verses*, contained several poems about Christ and the Virgin Mary, Pope Innocent VI, and poems about the Middle Ages inspired by an earlier visit to Bruges.

Although Ehrenburg managed to print only two hundred copies – he 'fasted for several months to save two hundred francs' – *Verses* did not go unnoticed in the Russian press.[3] The prominent poet Valery Bryusov, who had helped to found the Symbolist movement before the turn of the century, admired Ehrenburg's earliest work and even compared him to Nikolai Gumilev, one of the most acclaimed poets in Russia and the husband of the poet Anna Akhmatova. 'Among our young poets,' Bryusov wrote, '[Ehrenburg] is second only to Gumilev in his ability to construct verses and derive effect from rhyme and the combination of sounds... For now, images from the Middle Ages, the cult of Catholicism, a combination of religiosity and sensuality, gratify I. Ehrenburg, but he retells these old themes elegantly and beautifully.'[4]

Gumilev did not share Bryusov's enthusiasm. Writing in the influential St. Petersburg journal *Apollon*, Gumilev found little to praise. 'I. Ehrenburg has set himself a number of interesting goals: to reveal the face of the medieval knight who has by chance appeared amongst us; to express Catholic adoration of the Virgin Mary; to be refined; to create clear, expressive verse. But he has not remotely accomplished a single one of these goals since he does not possess adequate resources.'[5]

Encouraged by Bryusov's praise and undeterred by Gumilev's criticism, Ehrenburg continued to write. He published a second collection of verses, *I am Alive*, in St. Petersburg in 1911. Once again, Ehrenburg included several explicitly Catholic poems, along with verses about Paris and his nostalgia for Russia. Most interesting is his poem 'To the Jewish People,' his first public expression of concern for his fellow Jews. Despite his attraction to Catholicism, Ehrenburg still defined himself as a Jew and remained acutely aware of Jewish suffering. 'Alien and persecuted, you are not needed here/Gather your exhausted children/ And leave for the native fields of Jerusalem.'[6] This point of view underscores the poem's explicitly Zionist message: that the Jews have no place in Europe and should return to the land of Israel. It would not be the last time Ehrenburg expressed such an acute premonition.

Nikolai Gumilev read *I am Alive* and found encouraging improvement in Ehrenburg's abilities. 'I. Ehrenburg has made great progress from the time of his first book's appearance... He has passed from the ranks of apprentices and even, sometimes, steps forth on the path of independent creativity... Of course we have the right to demand still greater work from him, first of all in his language – but the most important thing is already accomplished: he knows what poetry is.'[7]

It was in 1914, however, with the advent of World War I that Ehrenburg embarked on a second literary career. He began reporting on life on the Western Front, submitting articles to newspapers in Petrograd.[8] It soon became apparent that he had a unique and compelling voice as a journalist. From that time on he never stopped writing – about politics, culture, and war.

Ehrenburg returned to Russia after the abdication of Tsar Nicholas II in early 1917 and was in Moscow when the Bolsheviks seized power in October. He had seen them up close in Paris and watched with dismay as they instituted a thorough-going dictatorship. He denounced the Bolsheviks in articles and poems in the Socialist Revolutionary press. His most notable collection of verse from those years, *A Prayer for Russia*, appeared in Moscow in early 1918. He expressed his despair in these poems, repeatedly depicting Russia as a woman who lies vulnerable, even naked, as violent men laugh and molest her.

Vladimir Mayakovsky decried *A Prayer for Russia* as 'tiresome prose printed in verses' and Ehrenburg as 'a frightened intellectual.'[9] But Ehrenburg's friend, the poet and literary critic Max Voloshin, wrote an enthusiastic review. Voloshin recognized the dimensions of Ehrenburg's life that made his work so compelling: he was a Jew, an émigré who had returned from France, an ex-Bolshevik. His status as an outsider helped to ensure a balance and spontaneity in his poetry that other writers lost in the face of their country's collapse. 'No Russian poet has felt the motherland's ruin with such intensity as this Jew,' Voloshin proclaimed. 'A Jew does not have the right to compose such verses!' – I once had to hear this exclamation about Ehrenburg's poem. It seemed to me the highest compliment to his poetry.'[10]

Ehrenburg's outspoken articles and verses led to his arrest. He was held briefly in a Moscow prison before Nikolai Bukharin intervened and gained his release. (Bukharin had befriended Ehrenburg in high school and inspired him to join the Bolsheviks as a teenager.) Still in Moscow, Ehrenburg joined the city's cultural ferment, enjoying new friendships with several leading poets, among them Boris Pasternak and Vladimir Mayakovsky. They read verses to each other and frequented the Poets' Café, where a writer could entertain an audience and receive a modest fee. By that time Alexander Blok was among the most revered poets in Russia. He, too, took notice of Ehrenburg, recalling the attitude of young people in a diary entry for January 31, 1918. 'First there were the three Bs – Balmont, Bryusov, Blok. Then they began to seem tame, and there was Mayakovsky. Now he seems tame as well, and there's Ehrenburg (he makes the most pungent fun of himself, and that is why, very soon, we shall all like no one but Ehrenburg.')[11]

Again with the help of Bukharin, Ehrenburg was able to leave Soviet Russia in 1922; he may have been the first private citizen to travel with a Soviet passport. His principal goal was to write a novel loosely based on his experiences in Paris, World War I, and the Bolshevik revolution. Although his poems and wartime journalism had made him well-known, this first novel established Ehrenburg as a provocative and unpredictable presence in Soviet literature, a status that endured throughout his life. Entitled *The Extraordinary Adventures of Julio Jurenito and His Disciples*, the novel is an extravagant satire taking aim at Europe's sacred myths and complacent assumptions about religion and politics, love and marriage, art, socialism, and the rules of war. The Bolsheviks are not spared either. In one famous chapter the Mephistophelian figure of Jurenito visits Lenin in the Kremlin and Lenin, without hesitation, expresses contempt for the Bolsheviks' opponents and vows to eliminate them all. Ehrenburg understood that the revolution was relying on coercion just as the tsarist autocracy had done before, and did not hesitate to say it.

Ehrenburg remained in Western Europe for nearly two decades, with only occasional visits to the Soviet Union. Reporting from various countries, he continued to write novels and eventually became *Izvestia*'s correspondent in Paris, earning a name for himself as an acute observer of the rise of fascism in Europe, even covering the Spanish Civil War. He was making his peace with the regime. For most of that time he stopped writing poetry until the shock of the Molotov-Ribbentrop Pact in August 1939 brought on a deep emotional crisis: Stalin was now allied with Hitler! Still in Paris, Ehrenburg lost the ability to swallow solid food for eight months – a profound attack of *anorexia nervosa*. His friends feared he was near suicide. It was then that Ehrenburg 'unburdened himself in poems:'[12] The question of loyalty lay at the heart of his personal crisis:

> Heart's the aim! Prepare to bear this weight,
> Faithful to your heart and to your fate.

It was only when the Germans made their advance toward Paris in May 1940 that Ehrenburg regained his equilibrium. He and his wife witnessed the Germans' entry into the French capital. As Soviet citizens they were now allies of the Germans, although out of an abundance of caution they took refuge in the Soviet embassy. Ehrenburg understood that the Soviet Union would not be spared by Hitler, the Pact notwithstanding. A Soviet patriot and convinced anti-fascist, he returned to Moscow by train through Berlin. Once in Moscow, Ehrenburg did what he could to alert the Kremlin to the Germans' intentions. His reputation as an anti-fascist initially hampered his ability to publish his novel *The Fall of Paris*, which described the German occupation. But then in April 1941 Stalin unexpectedly called him and assured Ehrenburg his book could appear. Nonetheless, Stalin chose to ignore warnings from Churchill and his own espionage agents, allowing Hitler to stage a devastating surprise attack on the Soviet Union on June 22, 1941.

Ilya Ehrenburg reached the height of his official prestige during the war. As a columnist for the *Red Star*, the newspaper for the Red Army, Ehrenburg took it upon himself to rally the troops and the country at large at a time when Hitler's Wehrmacht was driving deep into Soviet territory. He wrote nearly two thousand articles over the next four years, insisting that Soviet soldiers needed to hate the Germans in order to defeat them. He could be equally forceful in verse, as evident in the poem 'Kill' which can be found in this volume.

Ehrenburg also acutely felt the tragedy of his fellow Jews, for the Nazis murdered as many as two and a half million Jews in Soviet-occupied territory, an astonishing proportion of the six million who perished during the Holocaust. It was Ehrenburg, working alongside his fellow journalist Vasily Grossman and other Jewish and non-Jewish writers, who assembled hundreds of testimonies and documents about the Nazi massacres in German-occupied territory for *The Black Book*, a project that the Kremlin ultimately forbade to appear. He was the first to commemorate the Babi Yar massacre in a cycle of poems that appeared in Moscow in 1945. (And in 1948 his novel *The Storm*, which contained a vivid description of the massacre, received the Stalin Prize for literature.) But even as the war drew to a close with the allies reaching Berlin in April, Ehrenburg felt a resurgence of anxiety. 'More than likely it is in the nature of poetry to feel more sharply and deeply. I was not trying to be logical in verse. I was not comforting myself. I was expressing the bewilderment and alarm that lurked somewhere deep inside me.' In his poem 'Victory,' written on the night of the German surrender, Ehrenburg surprised himself with a sense of deep pessimism for the future:

> I longed for her as only lovers can.
> I knew her as the back of my own hand.
> I called for her, in grief, in blood, in lather.
> The time had come – war ended, finally.
> I saw her walking home, and she saw me.
> We didn't recognize each other.

His premonition was justified. With the advent of the Cold War the Kremlin's wartime alliance with the Western democracies broke down. Now Ehrenburg had to lend his rhetorical talents against a new enemy – the United States. He became a leading critic of American politics and culture in the Soviet press, as exemplified by his novel *The Ninth Wave (1951)*, one of the crudest books of his career and the only one he explicitly disavowed. Almost a parody of Soviet Cold War attitudes, the novel's message is that the Soviet Union represented the best hope for world peace, while craven American politicians, generals, and journalists pursue fantastic plots to undermine Communist achievements. And even as friends and fellow writers, including many Jews, suffered arrest and execution, Ehrenburg continued to travel widely. In January 1953 the Kremlin announced that a group of doctors, among them many Jews, had been conspiring to murder Soviet leaders. This was the notorious Doctors' Plot. The country was soon overwhelmed with suspicion toward Jewish doctors and there was even the palpable fear that the Kremlin would use the Doctors' Plot as a pretext to deport the country's Jews to Siberia. Ehrenburg, along with other prominent Jewish cultural figures, was called on to endorse the Kremlin's campaign. He was among a small handful to refuse to sign a collective appeal endorsing the Kremlin's plans – until he received a direct order from Stalin to sign. But even then he was the only person to send Stalin a letter explaining why an action against the Jews would be harmful to Soviet interests. In the end no collective appeal was ever published and with the dictator's death on March 5, 1953, his heirs soon publicly disavowed the Doctors' Plot.

Between Stalin's death and the emergence of Alexander Solzhenitsyn in 1962 Ehrenburg became the most recognized and acclaimed independent voice in the country, at the very center of debate and controversy. His novel *The Thaw* lent its name to that period of Soviet history. His essays on Chekhov and Stendahl were recognized as clarion calls against official censorship. He organized an exhibit of Picasso's work in Moscow in 1956, pushed through a Russian translation of *The Diary of Anne Frank* in 1960, and throughout the final decade of his life wrote and contended with the censors to see his panoramic memoirs, *People, Years, Life*, into print. Initially published in serial form in the prestigious, liberal-minded journal *Novy mir* (New World), which was edited by the legendary Alexander Tvardovsky, who also oversaw the publication of Alexander Solzhenitsyn's *One Day in the Life of Ivan Denisovich*, the memoirs restored the country's cultural history to a generation of readers who otherwise would never have known about hundreds of artists and writers, Soviet or European, whose lives and careers had been ignored, if not suppressed, for decades. Even a long, public denunciation of the memoirs by Nikita Khrushchev himself in March 1963, when Ehrenburg was threatened with arrest, did not compel him to back down. It helped him to overcome both advancing age and the effects of cancer, reinforcing the physical and moral stamina that set him apart from virtually all other cultural figures of his generation. No less a figure than Nadezhda Mandelstam came to his defense at that time. In a personal letter, she expressed her moral support for him with customary insight:

> From the point of view of everyday life it is hard to live in the epicenter of an earthquake. But in a certain sense this is important and necessary. You know there is a tendency to accuse you of not reversing the direction of rivers, of not changing the course of the stars, of not breaking up the moon into honey cake and feeding us the pieces. In other words, people always wanted the impossible from you and were angry when you did the possible.
>
> Now, after the latest events, it is obvious how much you did and are doing to relax our usual ways, how great your role is in our life and how we should be grateful to you. *Everyone* understands this now.[13]

Ehrenburg had resumed writing poetry in 1957, following a break of almost a full decade. As the target of Stalinist enforcers, who still held sway within the Party bureaucracy, he often employed Aesopian language to convey his intentions. On the surface his first poem from that time seemed to be about a change in seasons, about the rustle of leaves on a breezy morning, but it was really about the fate of his generation:

It was a usual quiet autumn day.
I could sit down to write – or not.
No love would take my peace of heart away.
No spot of trouble; not a spot.
The trees were stripping down and blackening –
My eyes, my window knew they were –
Made clear not by my clever reckoning,
But by the truths I knew before.
And then, cold wind blew in a startling blast.
Dead fallen leaves took off and flew.
Although they'd been downtrodden and downcast,
Like love, the leaves stayed pure and true.
So large, some yellow, some in orange hue,
Some with a silly greenish cast,
They didn't make it, yet they made it through,
And now I watch them flutter past.
How do they stay so spotless till the end?
Each word is weak or needs a tweak.
They are alive, but they have not been penned.
They flew up high, but they don't speak.

There is an echo of this poem in *People, Years, Life*: 'When I wrote about friends who are no more, I sometimes stopped working, went up to the window and stood there as people stand at meetings to honor the dead. I did not look at the leaves or at the snow drifts. I saw only the face dear to me.'[14] Haunted by their fate, he quoted poems of Marina Tsvetaeva and Osip Mandelstam that had never appeared in the Soviet press, a step that earned him the disdain of Stalinist critics who attacked him for wanting 'to drag out moldering literary corpses into the light of day and present them as something still capable of living.'[15] He could also be playful about his enthusiasms. When younger poets came to meet him, he would often challenge them to a game: to write down the names of their favourite ten poets in order, then compare the lists to each other's.

The poet Boris Slutsky, whose work Ehrenburg first championed in the late 1950s, recognized the unique power of

Ehrenburg's verses, complimenting him with an inscription in an old edition of Aesop's *Fables* that he presented to him as a gift. 'For the further perfection of your Aesopian language,' he wrote to Ehrenburg, 'with the help of the original.'[16]

After Khrushchev's removal from office in 1964, Ehrenburg could not ignore how his successors, led by Leonid Brezhnev, rolled back many reforms, leaving Ehrenburg depressed and discouraged that he would not live to see the flowering of cultural or political freedom in Russia. In one of his final poems, he expressed the poignant complexity of his life with remarkable candour:

Too late to cry, and the truth is not pretty:
I've lived a dog's life, and that's a pity.
Life wasn't too bad, just odd, and confusing –
Not that of a puppet, nor of a human;
Not that of a mensch, not of a true man.
I carried no lumber, but I've learned the trick
Of fetching my meaningless fetching stick.
I got no treats, and my masters hit me,
Yet I guarded the doors that wouldn't admit me.
Whenever the moon came out mean and scowling,
You'd hear me barking, you'd hear me howling;
I wasn't feral, I wasn't a stray –
I just was faithful enough to stay,
Not to my kennel and not to my stick,
Not to the dogfighters, hot and quick,
Not to sweet lies, not to street fights,
Not to vicious watchdog bites,
But only to weeping from my dark porch and
To my bed of straw, warm like misfortune.

Despite his ongoing treatment for prostate and bladder cancer Ehrenburg continued to write and travel. But by 1967 his health was deteriorating. A friend described him as severely changed. 'Wizened, balding, a yellow stain had broken out on his head, while his feet shuffled when he walked.'[17] His voice, once robust and clear, had shrunk to a barely audible whisper. On August 7, Ehrenburg suffered his first and only heart attack. He fell in the garden of his dacha outside of Moscow. Doctors were quickly summoned and for three weeks tried to counteract the damage. But he could not be saved. On August 31, the day after he was taken by ambulance to his Moscow apartment, his heart stopped beating as a nurse was taking his pulse. Ehrenburg was 76 years old.

Ehrenburg died at a moment when the regime was mounting a sustained campaign to enforce censorship, often resorting to trials of young activists who were challenging the Kremlin's controls of political and cultural expression. In the wake of his death the regime feared that crowds who were expected to gather in central Moscow to honor him might turn their grief over his death into a demonstration against censorship. So no announcements appeared in the press about the state funeral, which took place on September 4 inside the House of Writers, an impressive compound of buildings and gardens near Rebellion Square, in a neighborhood filled with embassies, including the American. That morning, U.S. officials were startled to see a crowd of fifteen thousand people – along with ten water trucks deployed nearby in case of trouble. An even larger crowd of twenty thousand tried to force their way into the grounds of the Novodevichy Cemetery to follow the casket to the grave. Nadezhda Mandelstam was among the mourners. 'There was a great crowd at his funeral,' she remarked in her memoir *Hope Abandoned*, 'and I noticed that the faces were decent and human ones. It was an anti-Fascist crowd, and the police spies who had been sent to the funeral in force stood out very conspicuously. It was clear, in other words, that Ehrenburg had done his work well, difficult and thankless though it was.'[18]

With these inspired translations of many of Ehrenburg's most significant poems the English-speaking world can begin to grasp what made him so necessary a voice in Soviet culture. We are indebted to Anna Krushelnitskaya for lending her considerable talent to this task.

Joshua Rubenstein

Notes

1. Ilya Ehrenburg, *Lyudi, Gody, Zhizn* (People, Years, Life) (Moscow, 1990) vol. 2, pp. 251–252.
2. Nadezhda Mandelstam, *Hope Abandoned* (New York, 1974), p. 16.
3. TSGALI, fund 1204, catalog 1, item 18.
4. From *Russkaya mysl* (Russian Thought), no. 2, pp. 232-33, cited in the commentary to *Sobranie Sochinenii* (Collected Works), vol. 1 (Moscow, 1990), p. 589.
5. *Apollon*, no. 5 (1911): p. 78. Gumilev then wrote to Bryusov objecting to the latter's praise of Ehrenburg. 'I found nothing in [his work] except for ungrammatical and unpleasant snobbism,' as cited in Boris Frezinsky and Vyacheslav Popov, *Ilya Ehrenburg, Chronika Zhizni i Tvorchestva* (Ilya Ehrenburg, A Chronicle of His Life and Work), vol.1, 1891-1923 (St. Petersburg, 1993), p. 76.
6. A full English translation of 'To the Jewish People' can be found in *Midstream* (April 1971): pp. 56–57.
7. Apollon, no. 10 (1911): p. 74.
8. The name St. Petersburg was changed to Petrograd at the outset of the First World War in order to give the capital a Russian name rather than a German-sounding one. After Lenin's death in 1924, Petrograd became Leningrad.
9. Cited in the commentary to Ilya Ehrenburg, *Sobranie Sochinenii* (Collected Works), vol. 1 (Moscow, 1990), p. 595.
10. Max Voloshin, *Russkaya mysl* (Russian Thought), no. 3430, September 16, 1982, p. 9.
11. Alexander Blok, *Sobranie Sochinenii* (Collected Works), vol 7 (Moscow, 1963), p. 324.
12. Ehrenburg, *Lyudi, Gody, Zhizn*, vol. 2, p. 218.
13. Nadezhda Mandelstam to Ehrenburg, following a public attack on him by Nikita Khrushchev in the spring of 1963. Archive of Natalya Stolyarova. Stolyarova was Ehrenburg's last secretary. She gave me a copy of this letter when I saw her in Moscow in May 1984.
14. Ehrenburg, *Lyudi, Gody, Zhizn*, vol. 3, pp. 259–260.
15. Vsevolod Kochetov, speech to the Twenty-second Party Congress, Pravda, October 31, 1961, p. 8.
16. As cited in Ilya Ehrenburg, *Stikhotvoreniya i Poemy* (Verses and Poems), edited by Boris Frezinsky (Saint Petersburg: Akademicheskii Proyekt, 2000), p. 62.
17. Yuri Oklyanski, *Schastlivie Neudachniki* (Lucky Failures) Moscow: 1990), p. 365.
18. Mandelstam, *Hope Abandoned*, p. 16.

Я скажу вам о детстве ушедшем, о маме
И о мамином черном платке,
О столовой с буфетом, с большими часами
И о белом щенке.
В летний полдень скажу вам о вкусе черники,
О червивых, изъеденных пнях
И о только что смолкнувшем крике
Перед вами в кустах.
Если осень придет, я скажу, что уснула
Опьяневшая муха на пыльном окне,
Что зима на последние астры дохнула
И что жалко их мне.
Я скажу вам о каждой минуте, о каждой!
И о каждом из прожитых дней.
Я люблю эту жизнь, с ненасытною жаждой
Прикасаюсь я к ней!

Март или апрель 1912

I'll talk of past childhood, of Mamma; I'll talk
Of the black shawl my Mamma wore up,
Of our dining-room hutch, of our grandfather clock,
Of our little white pup.
I'll talk of blueberries on a summer day,
Of tree-stumps, worm-ridden and dry,
Of the outcry that had just now died away
In the brambles nearby.
If it's autumn, I'll talk of the plastered
Fly sleeping in windowsill dust,
Of cold winter breath on my last summer asters –
I'm sad that they've passed.
I'll talk of each minute I lived, every minute!
Of each day I lived, last or first.
I love life, and I reach for everything in it
With unquenchable thirst!

March or April 1912

Мне никто не скажет за уроком «слушай»,
Мне никто не скажет за обедом «кушай»,
И никто не назовет меня Илюшей,
И никто не сможет приласкать,
Как ласкала маленького мать.

Март или апрель 1912

There's no-one to say, like back in class, 'stop acting funny!'
There's no-one to say when I have lunch,
'have seconds, honey!'
There's no-one to call me 'sweet Ilyusha, sonny'.
There's no-one to hold me like my Mamma did
Back when I was still a little kid.

March or April 1912

Как скучно в «одиночке», вечер длинный,
А книги нет.
Но я мужчина,
И мне семнадцать лет.
Я, «Марсельезу» напевая,
Ложусь лицом к стене,
Но отдаленный гул трамвая
Напоминает мне,
Что есть Остоженка, и в переулке
Наш дом,
И кофе с молоком, и булки,
И мама за столом.
Темно в передней и в гостиной,
Дуняша подает обед...
Как плакать хочется! Но я мужчина,
И мне семнадцать лет...

Март или апрель 1912

So bored in solitary, and the day won't end.
No books, I'm told.
But I'm a man.
I'm seventeen years old.
I lie in bed, my face against the wall.
I hum La Marseillaise.
But then, a distant streetcar call
Sings of the good old days
Back in Ostozhenka, of our small street,
Of our old home,
Of coffee served with cream and sweets,
And of my mum.
Now, in our hall and parlours, light is wan.
To dinner everyone is called...
So hard to hold back tears! But I'm a man,
I'm seventeen years old...

March or April 1912

Если ты к земле приложишь ухо,
То услышишь: крыльями звеня,
В тонкой паутине бьется муха,
А в корнях изъеденного пня
Прорастают новые побеги,
Прячась в хвое и в сухих листах.
На дороге вязнут и скрипят телеги,
Утопая в рыхлых колеях.
Ты услышишь: пробегает белка,
Листьями пугливыми шурша,
И над речкой пересохшей, мелкой
Селезень кряхтит средь камыша.
И поет бадья у нашего колодца,
И девчонки с ягодой прошли.
Ты услышишь, как дрожит и бьется
Сердце неумолчное земли.

Март или апрель 1912

If you press your ear down to the ground,
You will hear the droning of a fly
Struggling in a web to be unbound.
You will hear determined saplings pry
Through the roots of a decaying stump,
Hiding in pine needles and leaf mold;
Horse-drawn carts get stuck, and creak, and thump
Down the byways weatherworn and old;
You will hear a squirrel doing stunts,
Scurrying and rifling skittish leaves;
You will hear a mallard drake that grunts
By the shallow creek where bulrush weaves,
Buckets singing by the village well,
Berry-pickers calling back and forth...
You will hear the trembling, tolling bell
Of the dauntless heart of Mother Earth.

March or April 1912

О маме

Если ночью не уснешь, бывало,
Босыми ногами,
Через темную большую залу,
Прибегаешь к маме.
Над кроватью мамина аптечка –
Капли и пилюли,
Догорающая свечка
И белье на стуле.
Посидишь – и станет почему-то
Легче и печальней.
Помню запах мыла и уюта
В полутемной спальне...

Февраль или март 1913

About Mamma

On a sleepless night, when I felt restless,
I would scamper barefoot
Through the parlour's dark and empty vastness
To my Mamma's bedroom.
Here's my Mamma's bedside box of tablets,
Tinctures, liniments;
A flicker from a nearly-melted candle;
A footstool strewn with linens.
I would linger – then, I'd feel some hope;
I'd feel both sad and better.
Such a cozy smell of home and soap
Filled her dusky bedroom...

February or March 1913

Вздохи из чужбины

1 Плющиха

Значит, снова мечты о России –
Лишь напрасно приснившийся сон;
Значит, снова дороги чужие,
И по ним я идти обречен!
И бродить у Вандомской колонны
Или в плоских садах Тюильри,
Где над лужами вечер влюбленный
Рассыпает, дрожа, фонари,
Где, как будто веселые птицы,
Выбегают в двенадцать часов
Из раскрытых домов мастерицы,
И у каждой букетик цветов.
О, бродить и вздыхать о Плющихе,
Где, разбуженный лаем собак,
Одинокий, печальный и тихий
Из сирени глядит особняк,
Где, кочуя по хилым березкам,
Воробьи затевают балы
И где пахнут натертые воском
И нагретые солнцем полы...

Sighs from Abroad

1 Plyushchikha

I've been longing for Russia; my dreams
Were just dreams. I've been longing for naught.
I must pound foreign roads, and it seems
It is my inescapable lot!
I must wander around Place Vendôme,
Through the dull flat Jardin des Tuileries;
Lovestruck night haunts the streets that I roam,
Strewing streetlights through puddles with glee.
Like canaries that warble and chatter,
At the clock striking twelve, every day
Out of doors flocks of seamstresses scatter,
Each girl holding a charming bouquet.
Oh, to sigh for Plyushchikha, to drift
To the old lilac thickets that keep
An old manor, dejected, bereft,
Roused by baying dogs from its sleep;
To the sparrows waltzing in scores,
Spindly birches with birds overrun;
To the sweet-smelling wooden floors,
Shined with wax and warmed by the sun...

2 Девичье поле

Уж слеза за слезою
Пробирается с крыш,
И неловкой ногою
По дорожке скользишь.
И милей и коварней
Пооттаявший лед,
И фабричные парни
Задевают народ.
И пойдешь от гуляний—
Вдалеке монастырь,
И извозчичьи сани
Улетают в пустырь.
Скоро снег этот слабый
И отсюда уйдет
И веселые бабы
Налетят в огород.
И от бабьего гама,
И от крика грачей,
И от греющих прямо
Подобревших лучей
Станет нежно-зеленым
Этот снежный пустырь,
И откликнется звоном,
Загудит монастырь.

Март 1913

2 Devichye Polye

Tear by tear, tears are dripping
Stealthily from the roof.
Down the path you are slipping
On your ungainly hoof.
Ice that thawed not yet fully
Looks inviting and sly.
Strolling workingmen bully
Simple folk passing by.
A far-off monastery –
Past the main promenade –
And a sleigh-ride will carry
Riders back and then fade.
Soon this snow, no more driven,
Will surrender and yield.
With a cheer, peasant women
Will alight on this field,
And the chatter of women,
And the rooks' hearty caw,
And the sun kindly beaming,
Warm enough to bring thaw,
Will assure that these very
White fields turn celadon,
And the roused monastery
Plays its full carillon.

March 1913

Канун

На площади пел горбун,
Уходили, дивились прохожие:
«Тебе поклоняюсь, буйный канун
Черного года!
Монахи раскрывали горящие рясы,
Казали волосатую грудь.
Но земля изнывала от засухи,
И тупился серебряный плуг.
Речи говорили они дерзкие,
Поминали Его имена.
Лежит и стонет, рот отверст,
Суха, темна.
Приблизился вечер.
Кличет сыч.
Ее вы хотели кровью человеческой
Напоить!
Тяжелы виноградные гроздья,
Собран хлеб.
Мальчик слепого за руку водит.
Все города обошли.
От горсти земли он ослеп.
Посыпал ее на горячие очи,
Затмились они.
Видите – стали белыми ночи
И чернью покрылись дни.
Раздайте вашу великую веру,
Чтоб пусто стало в сердцах!
И, темной ночи отверстые,
Целуйте следы слепца.
Ничего не таите – ибо время
Причаститься иной благодати!»
И пел горбунок о наставшем успении
Его преподобной матери.

Февраль 1915

The Eve

A hunchback sang in the street.
Passersby hurried by, peering:
'I bow before you, the raging eve
Of a black year!
Monks rent their flaming robes,
Laying their hairy chests bare,
But the drought-cracked earth still groaned
And the silver plow dulled from the wear.
The speeches they made were brazen.
They worked in all names for Him.
Still, she lies moaning, mouth gaping,
Dry, dim.
Evening draws forth.
An owl knells.
You brought the blood of men for her thirst
To quell!
The bunches of grapes are heavy,
The wheat cropped and twined.
A boy leads a blind man around by the hand.
They've roamed far and wide.
A fistful of earth has turned the man blind.
He sprinkled the earth on his blistering eyes and
His sight is in a haze.
Look how the nights have whitened
And blackened the days!
Share your great faith left and right,
Until your hearts are hollow! Then,
Undefended against the dark night,
Kiss the blind man's footprints and follow them.
Keep nothing hidden – time for a mission.
A new sacrament is emerging!'
The little hunchback sang of the recent dormition
Of His Mother the Blessed Virgin.

February 1915

Прогулка

В колбасной дремали головы свиньи,
Бледные, как дамы.
Из недвижных глаз сочилось уныние
На плачущий мрамор.
Если хотите, я подарю вам фаршированного борова
Или бонбоньерку с видами Реймского собора.

«Ох вы, родные, хорошие!
Подсобите мне!...
Очень уж тошно
Без Митеньки!»
И на мокрых досках
Колыхался мертвый солдат,
Торчала горькая соска
В ярко-лиловых губах.
Нет, я поднесу вам паштеты,
А эти туши
Мы прикажем убрать астрами, только
фиолетовыми,
И вечером скушаем.
«Мальчик мой перебитый!...
Все переменится...»
Только ветер один причитывал:
«И презревши все прегрешения...»

Сентябрь 1915

A Stroll

Pig heads lay drowsing at the charcuterie,
Each pale like a dame in a girdle.
Their motionless eyes leaked despondency
Onto the weeping marble.
If you want, I'll give you a roasted hog stuffed with greens,
Or a box of bonbons painted with the Cathedral of Reims.

'Me-oh-my, I pray for relief!
I'm undone!...
Can't bear to breathe
With my Mitya gone!'
The dead soldier wobbled
On wet wooden strips;
An acrid plug stoppled
Someone's bright-fuchsia lips.
No, let me serve you terrine;
As to these remains –
We'll order them dressed in asters, dark-maroon,
To eat them as dinner entrées.
'My boy, my boy, mauled, maimed!...
Here come all new things...'
And the wind alone howled and wailed:
'And forgive us all our sins...'

September 1915

Молитва о России

Эх, настало время разгуляться,
Позабыть про давнюю печаль!
Резолюцию, декларацию
Жарь!
Послужи-ка нам, красавица!
Что не нравится?
Приласкаем, мимо не пройдем –
Можно и прикладом,
Можно и штыком!...
Да завоем во мгле
От этой, от вольной воли!...
О нашей родимой земле
Миром Господу помолимся.
О наших полях пустых и холодных,
О наших безлюбых сердцах,
О тех, что молиться не могут,
О тех, что давят малых ребят,
О тех, что поют невеселые песенки,
О тех, что ходят с ножами и с кольями,
О тех, что брешут языками песьими,
Миром Господу помолимся.
Господи, пьяна, обнажена,
Вот Твоя великая страна!
Захотела с тоски повеселиться,
Загуляла, упала, в грязи и лежит.
Говорят – «не жилица».
Как же нам жить?
Видишь, плачут горькие очи
Твоей усталой рабы;
Только рубашка в клочьях,
Да румянец темной гульбы.
И поет, и хохочет, и стонет.
Только Своей ее не зови –

A Prayer for Russia

Hey, come put your dancing shoes on!
Leave old sadness! Let's carouse!
Resolutions, declarations –
Burn down the house!
Give us some sugar, honey, we're there for it!
You don't care for it?
We'll pet you gently, you bet –
With the heel of a rifle,
With a bayonet!...
Then, we'll howl in dark despair
For all this sweet, sweet freedom!...
One and all, we'll offer a prayer
For our homeland and plead with Him.
For our fields of no grain, cold and gray,
For our hearts that are heartless,
For all those who don't know how to pray,
For those who tread on the helpless,
For those who merrily sing dreary songs,
For those who walk with stakes and knives bare,
For those who bark lies with their dog tongues
One and all, we will offer a prayer.
Lord, she's drunk, denuded, uncomely –
This is Your great country!
She tried to be merry, to forget the old hurt;
She drank, and she stank, and she sank in the dirt.
They say, 'she's not long for this world.'
What about our world?
See the bitter eyes of your worn,
Weeping humble servant;
Her shirt is tattered and torn,
Her dirtied cheeks fervid.
She cackles, she moans, she hums.
Just don't call her Yours –

Видишь, смуглые церковные ладони
В крови!
...А кто-то орет: «Эй, поди ко мне!
Ишь, раскидалась голенькая!...»
О нашей великой стране
Миром Господу помолимся.
О матерях, что прячут своих детей –
Хоть бы не заметили!... Господи, пожалей!...
О тех, что ждут последнего часа,
О тех, что в тоске предсмертной молятся,
О всех умученных своими братьями
Миром Господу помолимся.
Была ведь великой она!
И, маясь, молилась за всех,
И верили все племена,
Что несет она миру крест.
И, глядя на Восток молчащий,
Где горе, снег и весна,
Говорили, веря и плача:
«Гряди, Христова страна!»
Была, росла и молилась,
И нет ее больше...
О всех могилах
Миром Господу помолимся.
О тех, что с крестами,
О тех, на которых ни креста, ни камня,
О камнях на месте, где стояли церкви наши,
О погасших лампадах, о замолкших колокольнях,
О запустении, ныне наставшем,
Миром Господу помолимся.
Господи, прости, помилуй нас!
Не оставь ее в последний час!
Все изведав и все потеряв,
Да уйдет она от смуты
К Тебе, трижды отринутому,
Как ушла овца заблудшая

See her dark church-worthy palms
In blood and sores!
... Someone yells: 'Hey, come to me!
Come on, look at you all nekkid there!...'
For our great country
One and all, we will offer a prayer.
For all mothers hiding their sons –
Lord, have mercy!... Make the vultures be gone!...
For all who wait for their final hour,
For all who pray before death to be spared,
For all martyred at the hands of a brother,
One and all, we will offer a prayer.
Oh, but once she was so great!
She prayed through torment and loss.
All peoples thought that she would consecrate
The world in faith with the cross.
They looked to the East that was silent,
Grieving, vernal, iced,
And they said, believing and crying,
'Come, o the country of Christ!'
She lived, she grew, she prayed.
Now, she's no longer there...
For all the graves,
One and all, we will offer a prayer.
For those with a cross on,
For those with no cross nor a stone,
For the stones where our churches used to stand,
For snuffed candles, for mute belfries in disrepair,
For the new barrenness in our land,
One and all, we will offer a prayer.
Good Lord, have mercy! We trust in your power!
Don't abandon her in her final hour!
Let all trials and losses be past her,
Let her leave behind her apostasy,
Let her come to You
Whom she thrice denied,

От пахучих трав
На луг родимый!
Да отвергнет духа цепи,
Злое и разгульное житье,
Чтоб с улыбкой тихой встретить
Иго легкое Твое!
Да искупит жаркой страдой
Эти адовы года,
Чтоб вкусить иную радость
Покаянья и труда!
Ту, что сбилась на своем таинственном пути,
Господи, прости!
Да восстанет золотое солнце,
Церкви белые, главы голубые,
Русь богомольная!
О России
Миром Господу помолимся.

Ноябрь 1917

Like a lost sheep returns
To her home pasture,
Leaving tempting herbs!
Let her forsake her chains of spirit,
Her gleeful ways, evil and broken;
Let her smile softly and greet
Your weightless burden!
Let her atone for these hellish years
With passionate toil!
Let penance and hard work bring her
A different joy!
Lord, for her who strayed off her sacred path –
Spare your wrath!
Let the sun rise golden, the churches white,
The domes blue and fair,
Russia godly!
For Russia,
One and all, we will offer a prayer.

November 1917

Осенью 1918 года

О победе не раз звенела труба.
Много крови было пролито.
Но не растоплен Вечный Полюс
И страна моя по-прежнему раба.
Шумит уже новый хозяин.
Как звать его, она не знает толком,
Но, покорная, тихо лобзает
Хозяйскую руку тяжелую.
Где-то грозы прошумели.
Но тот же снег на русских полях,
Так же пахнет могильный ельник,
И в глазах собачьих давний страх.
Где-то вольность – далёко, далёко...
Короткие зимние дни...
Нет лозы, чтобы буйным соком
Сердце раба опьянить.
В снегах, в лесах низко голову клонят.
Разойдутся – плачут и поют,
Так поют, будто нынче хоронят
Мать – Россию свою.
Вольный цвет, дитя иных народов,
Среди русских полей занемог.
Привели они далекую свободу,
Но надели на нее ярмо.
Спит Россия. За нее кто-то спорит и кличет,
Она только плачет со сна,
И в слезах – былое безразличье,
И в душе – былая тишина.
Молчит. И что это значит?
Светлый Крест святой Жены,
Или только труп смердящий
Богом забытой страны?

Август 1918

Autumn of 1918

Fanfares of victories were played.
We witnessed bloodshed upon bloodshed.
Yet, the Eternal Pole stays icebound.
My country still remains a slave.
Now, her new master is a boorish loudmouth.
His name or rule she's yet to understand,
But she already offers slavish nuzzles
To her new master's heavy hand.
Somewhere, spring rainstorms came down hard.
Yet, Russia's fields are lost to the same snow.
Her air still smells like fir trees of the graveyard;
Her doglike eyes brim with the fear bred long ago.
There's freedom – far, too far away...
Short are these winter days...
No vine to yield the wild unruly grape
That rouses hearts of slaves.
In snows, in woods they bow down low.
They go back home – they sing, they cry.
They sing so plaintively, as though
They're giving Mother Russia her last rites.
The untamed flower of the foreign lands
On Russian soil just wilts and withers.
They brought that far-flung freedom here and then
They dressed her with a yoke and tethers.
Now Russia sleeps. We fight and cry out in her stead.
She only weeps when woken.
In her tears, no old apathy is shed.
The silence in her soul remains unbroken.
No words are spoken. Which means what?
Is hers a Holy Myrrh-Bearer's Cross,
Or simply a putrescent corpse,
A land that God forgot?

August 1918

Из желтой глины, из праха, из пыли
Я его вылепил.
Я создал его по своему подобию,
Плоть и кровь ему дал.
Я сделал ему короткие ноги,
Чтоб, земной, он крепко на земле стоял.
Я вручил ему меч возмездия и славы,
Чтобы он разил меня,
И сам его тем мечом окровавил,
Чтобы он походил на меня.
Я дал ему имя бренное,
Заставил его резвиться средь наших жасминов и роз,
И, чтоб мне презирать мою землю,
Я его на небо вознес.
И чтоб был он как слепой и безумный,
Чтоб огонь вовек не погас в аду –
Я припал к нему и в мокрую глину вдунул
Мой бушующий смутный дух.
А потом, взыграв, будто зверь веселый,
Молод, темен и слеп,
Высоко я занес мой торжественный молот
И землю отдал земле.
Господа нет, звери рычат,
Леса шумят.
В гробике розовом
Земле предают младенца,
И сыплются мертвые звезды,
Светлые, тленные.
Есть ветер,
И листьев трепет,
И шорох, и шелест,
И всхлип метели,
И моря рокот, ропот, волн топот,
И громы.

Out of yellow clay, out of dust, out of ashes
I molded my creation.
In my own image I made him.
Flesh and blood, I set him forth.
Short were the legs that I gave him,
So that he – of the earth – would keep to the earth.
I gave him the sword of revenge and glory,
So that he would smite me;
With that very sword, I painted him gory,
So that he would be like me.
I gave him an earthbound name,
I made him frolic amidst our roses and jasmines,
Then, to show the earth my disdain,
I raptured him to heavens.
Then, to blind him and turn him insane,
To keep flames of hell burning through ages,
I cleaved to him, and my breath livened up the wet clay
With my spirit turbid and raging.
Then, like a laughing beast full of swagger,
Young, dim, blind in my mirth,
I raised high my ceremonial hammer
And returned earth to earth.
There is no God; beasts are snarling.
Forests are stirring.
In a little pink coffin
A babe is consigned to the ground.
Dead stars keep dropping,
Lucid, earthbound.
There's only breeze
Flowing through trees,
Swishing, rustling,
Snowstorms gasping,
Seas rasping, misting, lisping,
And thunders,

И легкий прерывистый шепот
Влюбленных.
Есть только круженье, смятенье, вращенье,
В дикой и темной алчбе
Есть только время
И бег.

Между январем и мартом 1920

And the tremulous breathy whispers
Of lovers.
There's only reeling, bewildering, twining;
In dark savage greed and cunning,
There's only time
And running.

Between January and March 1920

Весна снега ворочала,
Над золотом Москвы
Шутя шумела клочьями
Внезапной синевы.
Но люди шли с котомками,
С кулями шли и шли
И дни свои огромные
Тащили, как кули.
Раздумий и забот своих
Вертели жернова.
Нет, не задела оттепель
Твоей души, Москва!
Я не забуду очередь,
Старуший вскрик и бред
И на стене всклокоченный
Невысохший декрет.
Кремля в порфирном нищенстве
Оскал зубов и крест –
Подвижника и хищника
Неповторимый жест.
Разлюбленный, затверженный
И все ж святой искус
И стольких рук удержанных
Прощальный жар и хруст.
Но верю – днями дикими
Они в своем плену
У будущего выкупят
Великую весну.
Тогда, Москва, забудешь ты
Обиды всех разлук,
Ответишь гулом любящим
На виноватый стук.

Март 1921
Москва – Рига

Spring pushed around her snowfalls.
Through Moscow's gilt skyline
She danced and played with torn shawls
Of sudden lazuline.
But people walked along with bags,
They walked and walked with sacks,
With hefty days they dragged like sacks
Behind their weary backs.
They turned the millstones of their thoughts;
They ground their worries raw.
No, Moscow! Your old soul was not
Made softer by the thaw.
I never will forget that queue,
That old hag's screechy plea,
That wall defaced with a brand-new
Half-ripped wet-inked decree.
The Kremlin's pauper porphyry,
All holy cross and teeth –
A telltale sign and offering
Of the zealot and the beast.
Abandoned and remembered,
Yet hallowed, that ordeal;
The heat and crunch of many
Hands held in a farewell.
But I believe – by suffering
Their savage days in bond,
They will buy back the great spring
That's to the future pawned.
Then, Moscow, you'll forget all pain,
All rifts and, like before,
You'll hum with love when I again
Knock meekly on your door.

March 1921
Moscow – Riga

Бой быков

Зевак восторженные крики
Встречали грузного быка.
В его глазах, больших и диких,
Была глубокая тоска.
Дрожали дротики обиды.
Он долго поджидал врага,
Бежал на яркие хламиды
И в пустоту вонзал рога.
Не понимал – кто окровавил
Пустынь горячие пески,
Не знал игры высоких правил
И для чего растут быки.
Но ни налево, ни направо, –
Его дорога коротка.
Зеваки повторяли «браво»
И ждали нового быка.
Я не забуду поступь бычью,
Бег напрямик томит меня,
Свирепость, солнце и величье
Сухого, каменного дня.

1939

The Bullfight

The burly bull came out surrounded
By crowds excited, cheering, raucous.
His big wild eyes looked out, confounded
And deeply sad, upon the gawkers.
The darts of hurt stung sharp like nettles.
He gave the foe a patient stare,
Ran charging at the bright muletas
And thrust his horns into thin air.
He had no clue whose blood it was
With which hot desert sands were glazed.
He knew no fighting rules or laws.
He never knew why bulls were raised.
Whether he ventured left or right,
His path was cut – that was the rule.
The gawkers shouted, 'Bravo! Fight!'
They waited for another bull.
I won't forget his heavy stride.
I'm vexed by his straightforward way,
The sun, the fury, and the pride
Of a rock-hard and bone-dry day.

1939

Русский в Андалузии

Гроб несли по розовому щебню,
И труба унылая трубила.
Выбегали на шоссе деревни,
Подымали грабли или вилы.
Музыкой встревоженные птицы,
Те свою высвистывали зорю.
А бойцы, не смея торопиться,
Задыхались от жары и горя.
Прикурить он больше не попросит,
Не вздохнет о той, что обманула.
Опускали голову колосья,
И на привязи кричали мулы.
А потом оливы задрожали,
Заступ землю жесткую ударил.
Имени погибшего не знали,
Говорили коротко «товарищ».
Под оливами могилу вырыв,
Положили на могиле камень.
На какой земле товарищ вырос?
Под какими плакал облаками?
И бойцы сутулились тоскливо,
Отвернувшись, сглатывали слезы.
Может быть, ему милей оливы
Простодушная печаль березы?
В темноте все листья пахнут летом,
Все могилы сиротливы ночью.
Что придумаешь просторней света,
Человеческой судьбы короче?

1939

A Russian in Andalusia

On pink gravel they conveyed the casket,
Haunted by a doleful bugle call,
Down a highway specked with startled hamlets,
Sprouting now a pitchfork, now a maul.
Rousted by the bugle music, songbirds
Whistled out their greetings of the day.
Scorched by heat and loss, the grieving soldiers
Walked unhurried on their solemn way.
He won't sigh for her who tried him sorely.
He won't ever bum a cigarette.
Fields were soft with drooping stalks of barley.
Picket-hobbled mules hee-hawed, upset.
Soon, a heavy tremor stirred the olives.
Soon, a spade assailed the stony ground.
No-one knew the name to call the fallen.
'Comrade' was the only name they found.
Now, the olive grove became a graveyard;
To his grave, a stone's the only guide.
What was childhood home to this one comrade?
Where the high clouds under which he cried?
Soldiers hunker; they can find no solace,
Swallowing the tears so hard to swallow.
Maybe, he liked birches more than olives
For their simple-hearted melancholy!
In the dark, all leaves will smell like summer.
In the night, all graves will look forsaken.
What is larger than the world or smaller
Than a human life so quickly taken?

1939

Не торопясь, внимательный биолог
Законы изучает естества.
То был снаряда крохотный осколок,
И кажется, не дрогнула листва.
Прочтут когда-нибудь, что век был грозен,
Страницу трудную перевернут
И не поймут, как умирала озимь,
Как больно было каждому зерну.
Забыть чужого века созерцанье,
Искусства равнодушную игру,
Но только чье-то слабое дыханье
Собой прикрыть, как спичку на ветру.

1939

A studious biologist, enraptured,
Investigates the laws of natural life.
He finds a very tiny rocket fragment;
No foliage must have stirred amid the strife.
Someday, they'll learn our age was terrifying.
They'll turn the troubling page and still remain
Unmindful of how winter crops were dying,
Of how much pain was brought to every grain.
Forget the musings of a future stranger;
Abandon the indifferent games of art;
Just shield somebody's fragile breath from danger,
A flame against a windstorm, with your heart.

1939

На ладони – карта, с малолетства
Каждая проставлена река,
Сколько звезд ты получил в наследство,
Где ты пас ночные облака.
Был вначале ветер смертоносен,
Жизнь казалась горше и милей.
Принимал ты тишину за осень
И пугался тени тополей.
Отзвенели светлые притоки,
Стала глубже и темней вода.
Камень ты дробил на солнцепеке,
Завоевывал пустые города.
Заросли тропинки, где ты бегал,
Ночь сиреневая подошла.
Видишь – овцы, будто хлопья снега,
А доска сосновая тепла.

1939

Read your palm – a map, where every river
Has been charted since your tender days,
Like the trove of stars that you've been given,
Like the pastures where your night clouds graze.
First, the wind was harsh and poised for slaughter.
Life seemed quick to wound you and to please.
You mistook serenity for autumn;
You were spooked by shadows cast by trees.
Trills are stilled in sparkling tributaries.
Now, your waters run both dark and deep.
You went breaking rock in sunbaked quarries.
You went seizing forts with naught to keep.
Now, the paths you've trod grew green and scruffy
And the periwinkle night is nigh.
Look – these sheep are snowflakes, white and fluffy;
Feel the warmth of this old slab of pine.

1939

Ты тронул ветку, ветка зашумела.
Зеленый сон, как молодость, наивен.
Утешить человека может мелочь:
Шум листьев или летом светлый ливень,
Когда, омыт, оплакан и закапан,
Мир ясен – весь в одной повисшей капле,
Когда доносится горячий запах
Цветов, что прежде никогда не пахли.
...Я знаю все – годов проломы, бреши,
Крутых дорог бесчисленные петли.
Нет, человека нелегко утешить!
И всё же я скажу про дождь, про ветви.
Мы победим. За нас вся свежесть мира,
Все жилы, все побеги, все подростки,
Все это небо синее – на вырост,
Как мальчика веселая матроска,
За нас все звуки, все цвета, все формы,
И дети, что, смеясь, кидают мячик,
И птицы изумительное горло,
И слезы простодушные рыбачек.

1939

You touched a branch; the branch awoke with rustling.
Like adolescence, its green sleep is guileless.
A consolation can be something trifling:
The song of leaves, the sunlit summer cloudbursts,
When, mourned, and sprayed with tears, and cleansed with showers,
The world shines in a single pendant droplet;
The wind broadcasts a potent scent of flowers –
Those flowers which you never knew were fragrant.
... I've seen it all – the years that fissure, injure,
The twisty roads of many misadventures...
A consolation can be hard to conjure!
Yet, I'll keep talking about rain and branches.
We'll win. The world will help with all its vibrance,
With all its sinew, every sprout and shoot,
With all this sky – too big for us in size as
A boy's new bright and cheerful sailor suit;
With all its sounds, with all its shapes and colours,
Its children playing ball, excited, beaming,
The intricate and stunning throats of songbirds,
The simple-hearted tears of fisherwomen.

1939

Додумать не дай, оборви, молю, этот голос,
Чтоб память распалась, чтоб та тоска раскололась,
Чтоб люди шутили, чтоб больше шуток и шума,
Чтоб, вспомнив, вскочить, себя оборвать, не додумать,
Чтоб жить без просыпу, как пьяный, залпом и на пол,
Чтоб тикали ночью часы, чтоб кран этот капал,
Чтоб капля за каплей, чтоб цифры, рифмы, чтоб что-то,
Какая-то видимость точной, срочной работы,
Чтоб биться с врагом, чтоб штыком – под бомбы, под пули,
Чтоб выстоять смерть, чтоб глаза в глаза заглянули.
Не дай доглядеть, окажи, молю, эту милость,
Не видеть, не вспомнить, что с нами в жизни случилось.

1939

Don't let me finish this, banish this voice, perish the thought, I beg,
So my memory breaks and my heartbreak cracks like an egg;
So people keep cracking loud jokes, more jokes, more racket;
So I wake with a start, stop myself, spy this thought and whack it;
So I crash through my life like a drunk falls asleep, swiftly facedown,
  alive but not kicking;
So the faucet keeps leaking at night, so the cuckoo clock keeps ticking;
So they drop, drop by drop, numbers, rhymes, anything, I'll take it;
So I can invent something tricky to make and then quickly make it;
So I battle the foe with a bayonet – only that against bombs, and not die;
So I stand up to death, proud and alive, looking him in the eye.
Don't let me see this through to the end, I beg, let me quit this,
Forget this, turn blind to the things to which we were victim and
  witness.

1939

Верность

Верность – прямо дорога без петель,
Верность – зрелой души добродетель,
Верность – августа слава и дым,
Зной, его не понять молодым,
Верность – вместе под пули ходили,
Вместе верных друзей хоронили.
Грусть и мужество — не расскажу.
Верность хлебу и верность ножу,
Верность смерти и верность обидам,
Бреда сердца не вспомню, не выдам.
В сердце целься! Пройдут по тебе
Верность сердцу и верность судьбе.

1939

Faithfulness

Faithfulness – a road that never winds.
Faithfulness – a trait of worthy minds.
Faithfulness – late August smoke and pride;
To the young, its burning is denied.
Faithfulness – together, guns we brave.
Side by side, we mourn a comrade's grave.
Sorrow, valor – we don't speak but feel,
Faithful to our bread and to our steel,
Faithful to our death and to our pain –
Undeclared, my heart-craze will remain.
Heart's the aim! Prepare to bear this weight,
Faithful to your heart and to your fate.

1939

Бродят Рахили, Хаимы, Лии,
Как прокаженные, полуживые,
Камни их травят, слепы и глухи,
Бродят, разувшись пред смертью, старухи,
Бродят младенцы, разбужены ночью,
Гонит их сон, земля их не хочет.
Горе, открылась старая рана,
Мать мою звали по имени – Хана.

Январь 1941

A great many Leahs, Haims, Rahels
Wander like lepers, ghosts of themselves,
Tortured by stones, blind, deaf,
Old women take off their shoes before death;
Newborns wander; night calls awake them,
Sleep won't take them, the earth won't take them.
Woe, the leaking wound of old trauma.
My mother's given name was Hana.

January 1941

Крылья выдумав, ушел под землю,
Предал сон и погасил глаза.
И подбитая как будто дремлет
Сизо-голубая стрекоза.
Света не увидеть Персефоне,
Голоса сирены не унять,
К солнцу ломкие, как лед, ладони
В золотое утро не поднять.
За какой хлопочешь ты решеткой,
Что еще придумала спеша,
Бедная больная сумасбродка,
Хлопотунья вечная душа?

Январь 1941

I made up wings and vanished underground;
I betrayed a dream and dimmed my eyes.
Like in slumber, it lies shot and downed,
A lustrous smoky-bluish dragonfly.
No, a siren's voice will not be smothered.
No, Persephone will not see light.
Icy-brittle hands will not be offered
To a gilded morning warm and bright.
Busy, in a tizzy, in a prison,
Did you set another hurried goal,
My possessed, unstable, lost to reason,
Never-quiet, ever-working soul?

January 1941

Есть в хаосе самом высокий строй,
Тот замысел, что кажется игрой,
И, может быть, начертит астроном
Орбиту сердца, тронутого сном.
Велик и дивен океана плач.
У инея учился первый ткач.
Сродни приливам и корням близка
Обыкновенной женщины тоска.
И есть закон для смертоносных бурь
И для горшечника, кладущего глазурь, –
То ход страстей, и зря зовут судьбой
Отлеты птиц иль орудийный бой.
Художнику свобода не дана,
Он слышит, что бормочет тишина,
И, как лунатик, выйдя в темноту,
Он осязает эту темноту.
Не переставить звуки и цвета,
Не изменить кленового листа,
И дружбы горяча тяжелая смола,
И вечен след от легкого весла.

1941

Chaos itself conceals an artful plan;
Its blueprint may seem like a game to man.
Perhaps, astronomers will deign to chart
The orbit of a sleep-inflected heart.
Grand is the sobbing of a sea storm-tossed.
First weavers took apprenticeship with frost.
A common woman's mournfulness will bide
Close to the tree roots and the evening tide.
There is a law for deadly stormy days
And for the potter dipping clay in glaze –
It's set by wheels of passion, and no fate
Accounts for birds in flight or foes at gate.
An artist has no freedom, so he will
Pay heed to words of stillness when it's still;
Like a sleepwalker walking in the dark
He'll touch and feel the darkness that is dark.
No sounds or colours can be rearranged.
The shape of maple leaves cannot be changed.
A friendship's heavy tar keeps hot for ever more,
Endless the wake behind a lightweight oar.

1941

Убей!

Как кровь в виске твоем стучит,
Как год в крови, как счет обид,
Как горем пьян и без вина,
И как большая тишина,
Что после пуль и после мин,
И в сто пудов, на миг один,
Как эта жизнь – не ешь, не пей
И не дыши – одно: убей!
За сжатый рот твоей жены,
За то, что годы сожжены,
За то, что нет ни сна, ни стен,
За плач детей, за крик сирен,
За то, что даже образа
Свои проплакали глаза,
За горе оскорбленных пчел,
За то, что он к тебе пришел,
За то, что ты – не ешь, не пей,
Как кровь в виске – одно: убей!

1942

Kill!

Like anger pulsing in your vein,
A year of blood, a stock of pain,
Like stumbling drunk on grief, not wine,
Like the dead silence of a shrine,
Which follows bullets and grenades,
Stays for a moment and then fades;
Like life – don't eat, don't drink, keep still,
No breath, no word, except for – kill!
For your unsmiling tight-lipped wife,
For your incinerated life,
For losing sleep, for crumbling walls,
For children's screams, for air-raid calls;
For, though an icon never cries,
Our icons have cried out their eyes;
For ravaged beehives; for the gall
With which he made his house-call;
For you – don't eat, don't drink, keep still –
Like anger in your temple – kill!

1942

Ненависть

Ненависть – в тусклый январский полдень
Лед и сгусток замерзшего солнца.
Лед. Под ним клокочет река.
Рот забит, говорит рука.
Нет теперь ни крыльца, ни дыма,
Ни тепла от плеча любимой,
Ни калитки, ни лая собак,
Ни тоски. Только лед и враг.
Ненависть – сердца последний холод.
Всё отошло, ушло, раскололось.
Пуля от сердца сердце найдет,
Чуть задымится розовый лед.

1942

Hatred

Hatred – a bleak January noon,
Ice and a clot of icebound sun.
Ice. Underneath, the river is frothing.
The mouth is clogged. The hand does the talking.
There is no more porch, no more chimney smoke,
No more warm woman's shoulder to stroke.
No kissing gate, no barking dogs outside.
No grief. Just the enemy and the ice.
Hatred – the final frost of the heart.
Everything's done, gone, and broken apart.
A heart-to-heart bullet will find its target.
A wisp will rise from the ice tinged with garnet.

1942

Есть время камни собирать,
И время есть, чтоб их кидать.
Я изучил все времена,
Я говорил: на то война,
Я камни на себе таскал,
Я их от сердца отрывал,
И стали дни еще темней
От всех раскиданных камней.
Зачем же ты киваешь мне
Над той воронкой в стороне,
Не резонер и не пророк,
Простой дурашливый цветок?

1943

There is a time to gather stones;
There is a time to scatter stones.
I've mastered all times through and through.
I've told myself: that's war for you.
I hefted stones; I came to part
With stones torn right out of my heart;
The darkness grew still more profound
With all the stones we scattered 'round.
Why do you nod and bow your head,
You, simple, silly flowerhead,
No prophet, no debater,
Above that gaping crater?

1943

Бабий Яр

К чему слова и что перо,
Когда на сердце этот камень,
Когда, как каторжник ядро,
Я волочу чужую память?
Я жил когда-то в городах,
И были мне живые милы,
Теперь на тусклых пустырях
Я должен разрывать могилы,
Теперь мне каждый яр знаком,
И каждый яр теперь мне дом.
Я этой женщины любимой
Когда-то руки целовал,
Хотя, когда я был с живыми,
Я этой женщины не знал.
Мое дитя! Мои румяна!
Моя несметная родня!
Я слышу, как из каждой ямы
Вы окликаете меня.
Мы понатужимся и встанем,
Костями застучим – туда,
Где дышат хлебом и духами
Еще живые города.
Задуйте свет. Спустите флаги.
Мы к вам пришли. Не мы – овраги.

1944

Babi Yar

My pen is weak, my words in vain.
Why write at all? My heart is heavy.
I'm hobbled with a ball and chain:
I drag the memories of many.
I lived in cities long ago.
Back then, the living were my brethren.
Now I dig up the dead; I go
Through graves in wastelands bleak and barren.
Yars, gullies, trenches near and far –
I'm right at home in every *yar*.
I think of kisses I was giving
To these sweet hands: my love, my wife –
Though, while I walked among the living,
I'd never met her in my life.
My child! My joy! My blushing braves!
My vast, enormous family!
Your voices come from shallow graves.
From underground you call to me.
We'll rise; we'll strain with all our might;
We'll rattle with our bones, exhumed,
Toward live cities filled with light,
With bread and sharp cologne perfumed.
Half-staff your flags. Blow out your stars.
We come to you – us gullies, *yars*.

1944

Когда я был молод, была уж война,
Я жизнь свою прожил – и снова война.
Я все же запомнил из жизни той громкой
Не музыку марша, не грозы, не бомбы,
А где-то в рыбацком селенье глухом
К скале прилепившийся маленький дом.
В том доме матрос расставался с хозяйкой,
И грустные руки метались, как чайки.
И годы, и годы мерещатся мне
Всё те же две тени на белой стене.

1945

When I was a young man, we were in a war.
I've lived a long life – we're again in a war.
Here's what I recall from that thunderous past:
Not a marching song nor artillery blast,
But a fisherman's hut holding fast to a rock
In a small fishing village next to the dock.
A sailor was bidding his woman farewell.
Her sad hands, like seagulls, soared and then fell.
Now years, it's been years, and still, I recall
Those two moving shadows upon a white wall.

1945

Я смутно жил и неуверенно,
И говорил я о другом,
Но помню я большое дерево,
Чернильное на голубом,
И помню милую мне женщину, –
Не знаю, мало ль было сил,
Но суеверно и застенчиво
Я руку взял и отпустил.
И все давным-давно потеряно,
И даже нет следа обид,
И только где-то то же дерево
Еще по-прежнему стоит.

1945

I lived my life unsurely, timidly.
I spoke of nothing that I knew.
But I will not forget that big old tree,
Black ink upon a field of blue;
A woman I was sweet on long ago –
And I'm not sure if I was weak –
I took her hand, and then I let it go:
A gesture diffident and meek.
It's all been lost, and many years went by.
I bear no grudge and no ill will.
And yet, somewhere, that tree is standing high.
Somewhere, that tree is standing still.

1945

Чужое горе – оно как овод:
Ты отмахнешься, и сядет снова,
Захочешь выйти, а выйти поздно,
Оно – горячий и мокрый воздух,
И, как ни дышишь, все так же душно,
Оно не слышит, оно – кликуша,
Оно приходит и ночью ноет,
А что с ним делать – оно чужое.

1945

A grief not your own is a gadfly:
You wave it off – it still hovers by.
You want to leave but you are too late.
Its air is humid and heavyweight.
You gasp for air but there is no breath.
The raving grief hears nothing: it's deaf.
It comes at midnight to keen and moan.
There is no cure – it is not your own.

1945

9 Мая 1945

1

О них когда-то горевал поэт:
Они друг друга долго ожидали,
А встретившись, друг друга не узнали
На небесах, где горя больше нет.
Но не в раю, на том земном просторе,
Где шаг ступи — и горе, горе, горе,
Я ждал ее, как можно ждать любя,
Я знал ее, как можно знать себя,
Я звал ее в крови, в грязи, в печали.
И час настал — закончилась война.
Я шел домой. Навстречу шла она.
И мы друг друга не узнали.

2

Она была в линялой гимнастерке,
И ноги были до крови натерты.
Она пришла и постучалась в дом.
Открыла мать. Был стол накрыт к обеду.
«Твой сын служил со мной в полку одном,
И я пришла. Меня зовут Победа».
Был черный хлеб белее белых дней,
И слезы были соли солоней.
Все сто столиц кричали вдалеке,
В ладоши хлопали и танцевали.
И только в тихом русском городке
Две женщины, как мертвые, молчали.

9 May 1945

1

They were lamented by a poet's pen:
They waited far too long to be together,
But then, they didn't recognize each other
In heaven, where they never hurt again.
While not in heaven, but upon this earth,
Where everything is hurt, and hurt, and hurt,
I longed for her as only lovers can.
I knew her as the back of my own hand.
I called for her, in grief, in blood, in lather.
The time had come – war ended, finally.
I saw her walking home, and she saw me.
We didn't recognize each other.

2

She wore a faded army uniform.
Her feet were bloody and her boots outworn.
She came and started rapping on the door.
Mother's at home, and dinner is at two.
'Your son and I served in one rifle corps.
My name is Victory. I came to you.'
Black bread turned white as day but lighter, sweeter.
Black tears ran tasting bitterer than bitter.
A hundred nations cheered and danced around.
They clapped their hands, and jubilation spread.
And meanwhile, in a sleepy Russian town
Two women kept the silence of the dead.

3

Прошу не для себя, для тех,
Кто жил в крови, кто дольше всех
Не слышал ни любви, ни скрипок,
Ни роз не видел, ни зеркал,
Под кем и пол в сенях не скрипнул,
Кого и сон не окликал, –
Прошу для тех – и цвет, и щебет,
Чтоб было звонко и пестро,
Чтоб, умирая, день, как лебедь,
Ронял из горла серебро, –
Прошу до слез, до безрассудства,
Дойдя, войдя и перейдя,
Немного смутного искусства
За легким пологом дождя.

1945

3

I beg not for myself – for them,
Who lived lives blood-soaked, and who then
Would never know a love, a harp,
A rose bouquet, a mirrored hall,
A homeward footfall crisp and sharp,
A soft and lulling slumber call –
I beg for rainbows and for dawn song,
For bells to ring, for blooms to float,
And for the day to sing its swan song
With silver trickling from its throat –
I beg in tears, my begging heart
Gone, woebegone and gone insane,
For some unutterable art
Hid by the hazy gauze of rain.

1945

Был тихий день обычной осени,
Я мог писать иль не писать:
Никто уж в сердце не запросится,
И тише тишь, и глаже гладь.
Деревья голые и черные –
На то глаза, на то окно, –
Как не моих догадок формулы,
А все разгадано давно.
И вдруг, порывом ветра вспугнуты,
Взлетели мертвые листы,
Давно истоптаны, поруганы,
И всё же, как любовь, чисты,
Большие, желтые и рыжие
И даже с зеленью смешной,
Они не дожили, но выжили
И мечутся передо мной.
Но можно ль быть такими чистыми?
А что ни слово – невпопад.
Они живут, но не написаны,
Они взлетели, но молчат.

1957

It was a usual quiet autumn day.
I could sit down to write – or not.
No love would take my peace of heart away.
No spot of trouble; not a spot.
The trees were stripping down and blackening –
My eyes, my window knew they were –
Made clear not by my clever reckoning,
But by the truths I knew before.
And then, cold wind blew in a startling blast.
Dead fallen leaves took off and flew.
Although they'd been downtrodden and downcast,
Like love, the leaves stayed pure and true.
So large, some yellow, some in orange hue,
Some with a silly greenish cast,
They didn't make it, yet they made it through,
And now I watch them flutter past.
How do they stay so spotless till the end?
Each word is weak or needs a tweak.
They are alive, but they have not been penned.
They flew up high, but they don't speak.

1957

Дождь в Нагасаки

Дождь в Нагасаки бродит, разбужен, рассержен.
Куклу слепую девочка в ужасе держит.
Дождь этот лишний, деревья ему не рады,
Вишня в цвету, цветы уже начали падать.
Дождь этот с пеплом, в нем тихой смерти заправка,
Кукла ослепла, ослепнет девочка завтра,
Будет отравой доска для детского гроба,
Будет приправой тоска и долгая злоба,
Злоба – как дождь, нельзя от нее укрыться,
Рыбы сходят с ума, наземь падают птицы.
Голуби скоро начнут, как вороны, каркать,
Будут кусаться и выть молчальники карпы,
Будут вгрызаться в людей цветы полевые,
Воздух вопьется в грудь, сердце высосет, выест.
Злобу не в силах терпеть, как дождь, Нагасаки.
Мы не дадим умереть тебе, Нагасаки!
Дети в далеких, в зеленых и тихих скверах, –
Здесь не о вере, не с верой, не против веры,
Здесь о другом – о простой человеческой жизни.
Дождь перейдет, на вишни он больше не брызнет.

1957

Nagasaki Rain

Nagasaki rain roves awoken, angered, manic.
A small girl clutches her blind doll in a panic.
This rain is unwelcome; the trees want it to stop.
Cherries come into bloom and right then, the blooms drop.
This rain is ashes seasoned with stealthy death.
The doll is blind, and the girl will turn blind next.
The child-size coffin will be contaminated,
Salted with lasting sorrow and lifelong hatred.
Hatred is like this rain: there's nowhere to hide.
Fish forget how to swim, birds how to glide.
Soon, every cooing dove will caw like a raven.
Every silent carp will start chomping and raving.
Every field flower will shoot out a poisoned dart.
Air will gnaw through your chest and suck out your heart.
Hate is hard as this rain from the sky on Nagasaki.
But believe us, we won't let you die, Nagasaki!
Kids playing in parks faraway, in quiet green spaces –
It's not about faith, or for faith, or even against faith.
It's all about human life, and life is all there is.
This rain will pass – and not a drop more on the cherries.

1957

Верность

Жизнь широка и пестра,
Вера – очки и шоры.
Вера двигает горы,
Я – человек, не гора.
Вера мне не сестра.
Видел я камень серый,
Стертый трепетом губ,
Мертвого будит вера,
Я – человек, не труп.
Видел, как люди слепли,
Видел, как жили в пекле,
Видел – билась земля,
Видел я небо в пепле, –
Вере не верю я.
Скверно? Скажи, что скверно.
Верно? Скажи, что верно.
Не похвальбе, не мольбе,
Верю тебе лишь, Верность,
Веку, людям, судьбе.
Если терпеть, без сказки,
Спросят – прямо ответь,
Если к столбу, без повязки, –
Верность умеет смотреть.

1957

Faithfulness

Life is broad and bright to the eye;
Faith is eyeglasses and blinders.
Faith moves mountains, but I –
I am a man, not a mountain.
Faith isn't my keeper or minder.
I've seen gray rock polished by
Worshippers' lips, no more coarse.
Faith wakes the dead, but I –
I am a man, not a corpse.
I've seen people go blind,
I've seen them live through a blaze,
I've seen the earth thrash and writhe,
I've seen skies of ashes – and I,
I have no faith in faith.
A mess? So say it's a mess.
A yes? So say it's a yes.
Not in swagger, not in prayer,
But I have faith in you, Faithfulness
To people, times, fates to bear.
What you must bear, grin and bear.
When asked, be an open book.
When burned at the stake with no blindfold to wear –
Faithfulness dares to look.

1957

Самый верный

Я не знал, что дважды два – четыре,
И учитель двойку мне поставил.
А потом я оказался в мире
Всевозможных непреложных правил.
Правила менялись, только бойко,
С той же снисходительной улыбкой,
Неизменно ставили мне двойку
За допущенную вновь ошибку.
Не был я учеником примерным
И не стал с годами безупречным,
Из апостолов Фома Неверный
Кажется мне самым человечным,
Услыхав, он не поверил просто –
Мало ли рассказывают басен?
И, наверно, не один апостол
Говорил, что он весьма опасен.
Может, был Фома тяжелодумом,
Но, подумав, он за дело брался,
Говорил он только то, что думал,
И от слов своих не отступался.
Жизнь он мерил собственною меркой,
Были у него свои скрижали.
Уж не потому ль, что он «неверный»,
Он молчал, когда его пытали?

1958

The Most Faithful

Two plus two was four; I didn't know it,
So the teacher marked my homework poor.
Then, I found myself in this big world where
Rules were many and rule-makers sure.
Rules would change but one thing would endure:
With dismissive smiles and much head-shaking,
Rule-enforcers marked my homework poor
For the same mistake that I kept making.
Teacher's pet was not among my titles.
I was not made flawless through my rearing.
Doubting Thomas, out of all disciples,
Seems to me to be the most endearing.
In his disbelief, he wasn't docile –
Myths and rumours constantly appeared!
I would venture more than one apostle
Warned the rest that Thomas should be feared.
He was not the brightest, our man Thomas,
Not a thinker, but a thorough doer.
Once he thought, he made his earnest promise.
Once he made it, he could not be truer.
Thomas had his set of sacred tablets,
His own yardstick, his own eyes and ears.
Maybe, it's because he was 'unfaithful'
He stayed strong while he was stabbed with spears.

1958

Да разве могут дети юга,
Где розы плещут в декабре,
Где не разыщешь слова «вьюга»
Ни в памяти, ни в словаре,
Да разве там, где небо сине
И не слиняет ни на час,
Где испокон веков поныне
Все то же лето тешит глаз,
Да разве им хоть так, хоть вкратце,
Хоть на минуту, хоть во сне,
Хоть ненароком догадаться,
Что значит думать о весне,
Что значит в мартовские стужи,
Когда отчаянье берет,
Все ждать и ждать, как неуклюже
Зашевелится грузный лед.
А мы такие зимы знали,
Вжились в такие холода,
Что даже не было печали,
Но только гордость и беда.
И в крепкой, ледяной обиде,
Сухой пургой ослеплены,
Мы видели, уже не видя,
Глаза зеленые весны.

1958

How could the children of the South,
Where roses dazzle in December,
Where 'blizzard' is a word that's found
Hard to decipher or remember;
How could they, under skies so blue
That never pale, that always blaze
Through endless summers, never new
From days of yore to nowadays,
How could they have a guess, an inkling,
On accident or in a dream,
If only for a spell, a twinkling,
Just how it feels to think of spring,
Just how it feels, when March is frigid,
When the despair becomes too much,
To wait and wait until the rigid
Unwieldy ice begins to budge?
Such winters keep our close acquaintance,
Such bitter colds we must abide,
That even sorrow wouldn't taint us;
All we possess is strife and pride.
So often, gripped in icy seething,
Through blizzards hiding everything
We looked out blind – and, without seeing,
We saw the greening eyes of spring.

1958

Я слышу все – и горестные шепоты,
И деловитый перечень обид.
Но длится бой, и часовой как вкопанный
До позднего рассвета простоит.
Быть может, и его сомненья мучают,
Хоть ночь длинна, обид не перечесть,
Но знает он – ему хранить поручено
И жизнь товарищей, и собственную честь.
Судьбы нет горше, чем судьба отступника,
Как будто он и не жил никогда,
Подобно коже прокаженных, струпьями
С него сползают лучшие года.
Ему и зверь и птица не доверятся,
Он будет жить, но будет неживой,
Луна уйдет, и отвернется дерево,
Что у двери стоит как часовой.

1958

I hear it all – the whispering, the whimpering,
The thoroughgoing catalogue of slights.
The war goes on; the sentry stands unwavering.
He'll stand there till the late midwinter light.
He might have his uncertainty and his own qualms.
The night is long; the trove of slights is deep.
But then he knows – the lives of his brothers-in-arms,
Just like his honor, are for him to keep.
There is no fate more bitter than apostasy.
A traitor lives a life that's not worthwhile.
Like flaking strips of skin, like scabs of leprosy,
His best years slither off him in a pile.
By no-one, bird or beast, will he be trusted.
He'll live but won't know living anymore.
The moon will leave; the tree will scoff, disgusted,
Unwavering, a sentry by the door.

1958

Коровы в Калькутте

Как давно сказано,
Не все коровы одним миром мазаны:
Есть дельные и стельные,
Есть комолые и бодливые,
Веселые и ленивые,
Печальные и серьезные,
Индивидуальные и колхозные,
Дойные и убойные,
Одни в тепле, другие на стуже,
Одним лучше, другим хуже.
Но хуже всего калькуттским коровам:
Они бродят по улицам,
Мычат, сутулятся,
Нет у них крова,
Свободные и пленные,
Голодные и почтенные,
Никто не скажет им злого слова –
Они священные.
Есть такие писатели –
Пишут старательно,
Лаврами их украсили,
Произвели в классики,
Их не ругают, их не читают,
Их почитают.
Было в моей жизни много дурного,
Частенько били – за перегибы,
За недогибы, изгибы,
Говорили, что меня нет – «выбыл»,
Но никогда я не был священной коровой.
И на том спасибо.

1964

The Cows of Calcutta

It is a true claim
That cows are not all the same:
Cows can be dairy, scary,
Lazy, named Daisy,
With eyes full of laughs or eyes full of grief,
Kept for calving, kept for beef,
With long horns, with no horns,
Owned by a person or a kolkhoz,
Fed poorly or fed well,
In hog heaven or in cow hell.
Calcutta cows are the saddest cows:
They browse, they drowse,
They moo, they roam –
They have no home.
Unfree, liberated,
Worshipped, unsated,
Not raising any eyebrows –
They are sacred.
There are writers like that, you see –
They write assiduously;
They are venerated;
They are decorated;
They are never berated or read –
They are revered instead.
My own bitter cup was a tankful.
I got beaten for each overreach,
Underreach, careless speech.
I was told there was no more me – 'gone now.'
But I never was a sacred cow,
For which I'm thankful.

1964

Морили прежде в розницу,
Но развивались знания.
Мы, может, очень поздние,
А может, слишком ранние.

Сидел писец в Освенциме,
Считал не хуже робота —
От матерей с младенцами
Волос на сколько добыто.

Уж сожжены все родичи,
Канаты все проверены,
И вдруг пустая лодочка
Оторвалась от берега,
Без виз, да и без физики,
Пренебрегая воздухом,
Она к тому приблизилась,
Что называли звездами.

Когда была искомая
И был искомый около,
Когда еще весомая
Ему дарила локоны.
Одна звезда мне нравится.
Давно такое видано,
Она и не красавица,
Но очень безобидная.

Там не снует история,
Там мысль еще не роздана,
И видят инфузории
То, что зовем мы звездами.

Old deaths came at a slower rate.
For slaughter, science was a boon.
Perhaps we have arrived too late.
Perhaps we have arrived too soon.

An Auschwitz scribe reflected on
Net pay for every instance
Of hair in bulk collected from
Dead mothers and their infants.

Your every relative's been burned,
Strong every knot and lock;
But then, a lightweight empty boat
Sails swiftly off the dock.
No visas and no physics,
By the atmosphere unbarred,
It sails up high and visits
What they called heavens starred.

When the desired entity
Met her desired entity,
She still had her solidity;
She gave him lockets giddily.
I like one star among them all –
A story old but timeless –
It's not exactly beautiful,
But it is very harmless.

It has no trace of history.
It rests by thought unmarred,
And infusoria get to see
What we call heavens starred.

Лети, моя любимая!
Так вот оно, бессмертие, –
Не высчитать, не вымолвить,
Само собою вертится.

1964

Fly off, o my desired one!
So this is immortality –
No uttered words, no numbers run;
A perpetuum mobile.

1964

Последняя любовь

Календарей для сердца нет,
Все отдано судьбе на милость.
Так с Тютчевым на склоне лет
То необычное случилось,
О чем писал он наугад,
Когда был влюбчив, легкомыслен,
Когда, исправный дипломат,
Был к хаоса жрецам причислен.
Он знал и молодым, что страсть
Не треск, не звезды фейерверка,
А молчаливая напасть,
Что жаждет сердце исковеркать.
Но лишь поздней, устав искать,
На хаос наглядевшись вдосталь,
Узнал, что значит умирать
Не поэтически, а просто.
Его последняя любовь
Была единственной, быть может.
Уже скудела в жилах кровь
И день положенный был прожит.
Впервые он узнал разор,
И нежность оказалась внове...
И самый важный разговор
Вдруг оборвался на полслове.

1965

Last Love

There are no seasons for the heart:
It's tossed by winds that fate will summon.
Tyutchev's was pierced by a strange dart
In his old age – a love uncommon
He had divined back in the day
When he was fickle, young, flirtatious,
When he, a skillful attaché,
Was counted as a priest of chaos.
A young man, he already knew
That passion isn't stars and sparklers
But an affliction, rude and mute,
That mars the heart, and so is heartless.
Much later when his jaded eye
Had witnessed chaos good and plenty
He found out what it means to die,
Die not poetically, but plainly.
Perhaps, for him, this late last love
Proved to be singular and true.
His slowing heart no longer strove.
The days ordained for him were through.
For once, he felt the devastation;
For once, he fell to tenderness...
But this momentous conversation
Was halted and then broke mid-breath.

1965

В Доме литераторов

Для золота – старатели,
Для полок – собиратели,
Для школ – преподаватели,
Чтоб знали то и то,
Но для чего писатели,
Не ведает никто.
Завалены заказами,
Классическими фразами
Иль, ударяясь в стих,
Умеют пересказывать,
Что сделано до них.
Пораспрощался с музами,
Ну чем тебе не бог,
И хоть не связан узами,
Но знает свой шесток.
Оракулы, ораторы,
Оратели и патеры
Кричат про экскаваторы
И прославляют труд
В том Доме литераторов,
Где и богов секут.
Исхлестаны, взлелеяны,
Подкованы, подклеены,
Вдыхают юбилеями
Душистый дерматин,
И каждому по блеянью
Положен сан и чин.
Но вот поэту томному,
Прозаику скоромному
Старуха шепчет «стоп».

At the House of Writers

Miners are meant for mining ore,
Grocers are meant to mind the store,
Teachers are meant to teach and bore
Their pupils, more or less.
But what we're keeping writers for –
That's anybody's guess.
So busy are their business days;
They've mastered classical cliches;
Employing verse – or not –
They give a novel turn of phrase
To stale and stolen thought.
A writer bade his Muse goodbye –
A state of godlike grace!
Although he claims no ties that tie,
He knows his rightful place.
Inciters and igniters,
Pontificators, biters
Shout of tractors and firefighters,
Praising workers by the script
Inside that House of Writers
Where even gods get whipped.
They have been flogged, they have been beat,
They have been trained and tossed a treat;
They take in lungfuls of the sweet,
Prestigious leatherette.
They must compete in how they bleat
For crowns and ranks they get.
A poet, languorous of mood,
A novelist, well-fed and lewd,
Gets flagged by the grim reaper.

Приносят в дом тот, в комнату,
Двуличен был, в огромную,
Был высечен, – в укромную –
Вполне приличный гроб.
У ног иль изголовия
С глазищами коровьими
Становятся друзья,
Один принес пословицу,
Другому нездоровится,
А третьему нельзя.
Четвертый молвит вежливо:
«Скажи, любимый, где же ты?
Уж нет зубов для скрежета
И скорбь легла на грудь.
Мы будем жить по-прежнему,
А ты, назло всей нежити,
Ступай в последний путь!
Мы из того же семени,
Мы все пойдем за премией,
Как ты ходил вчера.
Иди путями теми... Нет,
Тебе уж спать пора!»

1966

To spacious rooms where he pursued
(He had been flayed) – his quietude –
A coffin's brought – (he played a prude) –
Of certain price, no cheaper.
His cow-eyed friends come out to meet
Right by his head or by his feet;
They line up in a chain.
The first one's reading off a sheet;
The second needs a bite to eat;
The third one must abstain.
The fourth one says, prim like a nun,
'Our dear beloved, where've you gone?
We'd gnash our teeth, but we have none.
Our garments we must rip.
We'll live like we have always done.
You hurry, not to be outrun,
Off on your final trip!
We be of one blood. In accord,
We're off to chase the same award
As you did. You must keep
To paths you've made... Oh, no! Abort!
It's time for you to sleep.'

1966

Зверинец

Приснилось мне, что я попал в зверинец,
Там были флаги, вывески гостиниц,
И детский сад, и древняя тюрьма,
Сновали лифты, корчились дома,
Но не было людей. Огромный боров
Жевал трико наездниц и жонглеров,
Лишь одряхлевший рыжий у ковра
То всхлипывал, то восклицал «ура».
Орангутанг учил дикообраза,
Что иглы сделаны не для показа,
И, выполняя обезьяний план,
Трудился оскопленный павиан.
Шакалы в страхе вспоминали игры
Усатого замызганного тигра,
Как он заказывал хороший плов
Из мяса дрессированных волков,
А поросята «с кашей иль без каши»
На вертел нацепляли зад мамаши.
Над гробом тигра грузный бегемот
Затанцевал, роняя свой живот,
Сжимал он грозди звезд в коротких лапах
И розы жрал, хоть осуждал их запах.
Потом прогнали бегемота прочь
И приказали воду истолочь.
«Который час?» – проснулся я, рыдая,
Состарился, уж голова седая.
Очнуться бы! Вся жизнь прошла, как сон.
Мяукает и лает телефон:
«Доклад хорька: луну кормить корицей»,
«Все голоса курятника лисице»,
«А носорог стал богом на лугу».
Пусть бог, пусть рог. Я больше не могу!

1966

The Menagerie

I dreamed I was in a menagerie.
It had flags, pennants, a hotel marquee,
A kindergarten and an ancient jail.
Trains raced and buildings towered without fail.
No people were in sight. A hog chewed hard
On a plate-spinner's circus leotard.
A relic of a clown used his beret
To wipe his tears, and then to wave hooray.
A porcupine was taught by a baboon
That needles are an asset and a boon.
A gelded yet enthused orangutan
Worked hard to meet his great-ape five-year plan.
With trepidation, jackals would rehash
Pranks of the tiger with a frayed mustache,
Who'd take his pick of trained wolves from the zoo,
Then have them seasoned for a hearty stew.
Meanwhile, three suckling piglets, pink and plump,
Squealed skewering their mother's ample rump.
A hippo danced around the tiger's tomb.
His belly wobbled and his feet went boom.
He crushed star clusters in his stubby paws,
Cursed roses, and then ate them from the vase.
Then, orders came to have him sent away
And have all water ground by end of day.
'What time is it?' I cried out in the night.
My face was streaked with tears; my hair was white.
Oh, to wake up! My life was but a dream.
Bleats on my phone come in a steady stream:
'The weasel says to feed the moon with rocks!'
'All henhouse votes go to elect the fox!'
'The warthog is now Wart-God! So be it!'
A god, a hog, a dog. I'm done! I quit.

1966

Из поэмы «Старость»

Пора признать – хоть вой, хоть плачь я,
Но прожил жизнь я по-собачьи,
Не то что плохо, а иначе, –
Не так, как люди или куклы,
Иль Человек с заглавной буквы:
Таскал не доски, только в доску
Свою дурацкую поноску,
Не за награды – за побои
Стерег закрытые покои,
Когда луна бывала злая,
Я подвывал и даже лаял
Не потому, что был я зверем,
А потому, что был я верен –
Не конуре, да и не палке,
Не драчунам в горячей свалке,
Не дракам, не красивым вракам,
Не злым сторожевым собакам,
А только плачу в темном доме
И теплой, как беда, соломе.

1966

from 'Old Age'

Too late to cry, and the truth is not pretty:
I've lived a dog's life, and that's a pity.
Life wasn't too bad, just odd, and confusing –
Not that of a puppet, nor of a human;
Not that of a mensch, not of a true man.
I carried no lumber, but I've learned the trick
Of fetching my meaningless fetching stick.
I got no treats, and my masters hit me,
Yet I guarded the doors that wouldn't admit me.
Whenever the moon came out mean and scowling,
You'd hear me barking, you'd hear me howling;
I wasn't feral, I wasn't a stray –
I just was faithful enough to stay,
Not to my kennel and not to my stick,
Not to the dogfighters, hot and quick,
Not to sweet lies, not to street fights,
Not to vicious watchdog bites,
But only to weeping from my dark porch and
To my bed of straw, warm like misfortune.

1966

Notes

The source for all originals included in this collection is: Ilya Ehrenburg. *Sobranie Sochinenii* (Collected Works), vol. 1 (Moscow, 1990).

Autumn of 1918
This poem contains an allusion to Fyodor Tyutchev's poem '14 December 1825' dedicated to the failed Decembrist Revolt in tsarist Russia; see excerpt in Robert Chandler's translation, quoted from *The Penguin Book of Russian Poetry* (Penguin Classics, 2015), p. 104:

> 'O sacrifice to reckless thought,
> it seems you must have hoped
> your scanty blood had power enough
> to melt the eternal Pole.
> A puff of smoke, a silent flicker
> upon the age-old ice –
> and then a breath of iron winter
> extinguished every trace.'

Babi Yar
The two-day mass shooting of Jews at a ravine called Babi Yar (or Babyn Yar) in 1941 was one of the largest massacres perpetrated by German Nazis in Europe during WW2.

The Cows of Calcutta
Although the city's name is now Anglicized as Kolkata to match the Bengali pronunciation, we elected to use the obsolete spelling contemporary to Ehrenburg's writing.

Last Love
Here, Ehrenburg refers to the 1852 poem by Fyodor Tyutchev entitled 'Last Love'; see first stanza, tr. Robert Chandler, *The Penguin Book of Russian Poetry* (Penguin Classics, 2015), p. 109:

'Towards our end, as life runs out,
love is more troubled and more tender.
Fade not, fade not, departing light
of our last love, our farewell splendour.'

Ehrenburg wrote his own 'Last Love' as a tribute to Liselotte Mehr, his devoted companion for the final fifteen years of his life. Her husband was Hjalmar Mehr, the Mayor of Stockholm and the most successful Jewish politician in Swedish history. She helped to arrange medical treatment for Ehrenburg in Stockholm after he was diagnosed with prostate and bladder cancer in the late 1950s.

At the House of Writers
The Central House of Writers (Tsentralnii Dom Literatorov, or TsDL) on Povarskaya St. in Moscow housed an administrative building, meeting spaces and a restaurant of the Union of Soviet Writers since 1934. In this poem, Ehrenburg satirizes the currying of favors, jockeying for position and infighting characteristic of the Union of Writers' internal politics of the time.

Acknowledgements

The translator extends her abiding gratitude to fellow translator Dmitri Manin, whose collegial advice is always available and always appreciated.